flutter

fly

scary

creepy

The Usborne
First
Illustrated
Thesaurus

noisy

loud

bang bang!

Jane Bingham
and Caroline Young

Illustrated by
Tjarda Borsboom
and Beatrice Tinarelli

gigantic

massive

Edited by
Felicity Brooks

Designed by
Kirsty Tizzard

speed

zoom

Using this book

A thesaurus is a book that groups together words with the same or similar meanings. You can use it to find words to make your writing and speaking more interesting. So you can change this:

My friends are nice.
We went to a nice party
and had a nice time.

to this:

My friends are great. We
went to a fantastic party
and had a wonderful time.

This thesaurus is divided into topics. You can search through the book to find a topic you want, or check the contents on pages 4 and 5.

Look at the words and pictures to give you ideas.

Find a range of words to make your writing more varied.

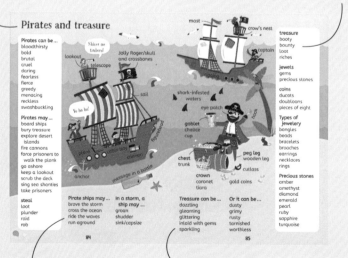

Discover striking phrases.

Choose from a list of interesting words to describe things.

Using the word finder

If you want to find other ways to say a particular word, use the word finder on pages 96 to 104.
It is in alphabetical order, so to find the word 'nice', look under 'n'.

The word finder will help you choose a word.

nervous, 18

nice, 6

noise, 81

The word finder tells you to look on page 6 to find other words that mean 'nice'.

Choosing words

Each time you write or speak, you make choices about words. Here are some ways to use words to create dramatic effects.

Make people come to life by showing how they look, sound and act.

The pirate had <u>flowing hair</u> and a <u>menacing grin</u>. He gave an <u>evil cackle</u> as he <u>waved</u> his hook.

Describe how places look, sound, feel, and even smell.

Parrots <u>screeched</u> in the <u>dark</u>, <u>steamy</u> jungle, and the air was filled with the <u>scent</u> of flowers.

Create a sense of speed and movement by using lots of action words.

The spaceship <u>zoomed</u> through the clouds, <u>hurtled</u> past the planet and <u>raced</u> away.

Contents

soar
swoop
fast
quick
hurry
rush

4

colorful

bright

jolly

happy

content

stroll

walk

Good, bad, nice

A good artist
expert
gifted
skillful
talented

A good child
angelic
obedient
polite
well-behaved

A good book
fantastic
excellent
marvelous
wonderful

A bad person
cruel
evil
nasty
wicked

Bad behavior
disobedient
mischievous
naughty
ornery

A bad smell
disgusting
horrible
revolting
vile

A nice time
amazing
fantastic
great
wonderful

A nice view
beautiful
breathtaking
spectacular
stunning

A nice person
caring
helpful
kind
warm-hearted

Big and small

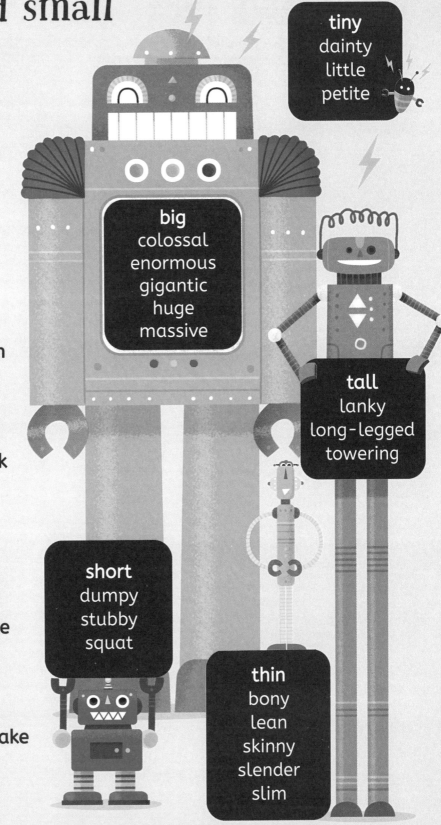

A big person
beefy
fat
heavy
hefty
large
overweight

A big lake
immense
vast
wide

A big decision
important
major
serious

A small speck
microscopic
minute
teensy
teeny
tiny

A small space
cramped
narrow
tight

A small mistake
minor
slight
unimportant

tiny
dainty
little
petite

big
colossal
enormous
gigantic
huge
massive

tall
lanky
long-legged
towering

short
dumpy
stubby
squat

thin
bony
lean
skinny
slender
slim

Colors

Colors can be ...

dark
deep

light
pale

bright
bold
brilliant
fluorescent
garish
luminous
rich
vivid

dull
dingy
drab
dreary
faded
faint
muddy

More colors
beige
black
brown
cream
fawn
hazel
ivory
khaki

yellow
lemon
mustard

red
crimson
ruby
scarlet

pink
coral
rose pink
salmon pink

white

gray
charcoal
dove gray

blue
navy
royal blue
sky blue
turquoise

orange
amber
apricot
peach

green
bottle green
emerald green
lime green
olive green

violet
lavender
lilac
mauve

purple
maroon
plum

8

Shapes and patterns

Shapes can be...
hexagonal
rectangular
square
triangular

round
circular
globular
spherical

flat
level
smooth

pointed
sharp
spiky

long
stretched-out

short
squat

Flat shapes

edge/side

circle   square   triangle

oval   diamond   rectangle

pentagon   hexagon   octagon

Solid shapes

corner   point

sphere   cone   cube   pyramid

Patterns can be...
bold
delicate
eye-catching
floral
flowing
random
regular
swirling

stripes   plaid

zigzags   spots/polka dots   spirals

Describing faces

Faces can be ...
heart-shaped
long
round

good-looking
attractive
beautiful
handsome
pretty

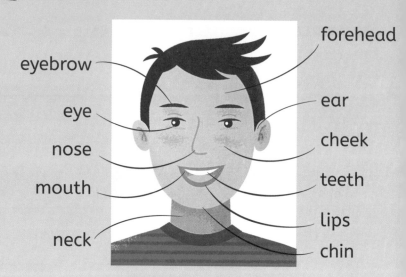

forehead
eyebrow
eye
nose
mouth
neck
ear
cheek
teeth
lips
chin

Faces can have ...

glasses

wrinkles   freckles   a beard   braces

stubble   pimples   a mustache   dimples

People may ...

grin   smile   frown   blush

Hair and hairstyles

Hair can be...
curly
flowing
frizzy
greasy
lank
limp
receding
shiny
sleek
spiky
straggly
straight
windswept
wiry

thick
bushy
shaggy

thin
fine
thinning
wispy

Hair may be...
bleached
dyed
gelled
layered
permed
shaved
slicked back
spiked
tinted

Hair colors
auburn
black
blonde
brown
chestnut
fair
gray
mousy
red
silver
strawberry blonde
white

Hairstyles
bob
bun
crew cut
dreadlocks
mohawk
pixie cut
ponytail
quiff
ringlets
top knot

Other hair words
bald patch
barrette
hair clip
hair extension
headband
sideburns
wig

bun
bangs
part
pigtail
cornrows
tangled
wavy
braids

11

Clothes and shoes

wool

pleats

undershirt

raincoat

T-shirt

tights

sweater

skirt

Coats
duffle coat
jacket
parka
trench coat

Hats
baseball cap
beanie
beret
sunhat
top hat
wool

Dresses
party dress
sundress
tunic

Pants
jogging bottoms
leggings
shorts

Underwear
boxer shorts
bra
briefs
panties
underpants

Tops
cardigan
hoodie
shirt
sweater
sweatshirt

Nightclothes
bathrobe
nightdress/
  nightie
pajamas
slippers

Other clothes
bodysuit
gloves
mittens
scarf
socks
suit
tie
tracksuit
vest

Shoes and boots

canvas

flip-flops

sandals

pumps

rubber boots

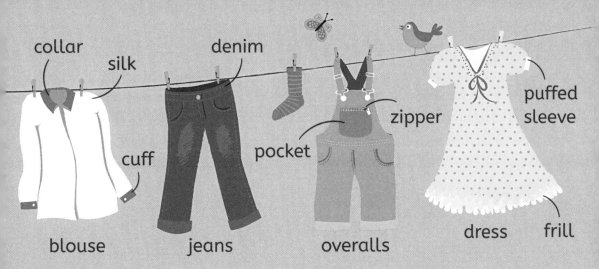

collar

silk

denim

zipper

puffed sleeve

cuff

pocket

dress   frill

blouse   jeans   overalls

Clothes can be made from ...
corduroy
cotton
fur
lace
satin
velvet

Some clothes have ...
buttons
fringe
patches
ruffles
sequins
tassels

Clothes can be ...
neat
ironed
tidy

scruffy
frayed
shabby
ragged

tight
clingy

loose
baggy

flowing
floating

dirty
grubby
muddy
stained

They can also be ...
comfortable
elegant
fancy
fashionable
fun
plain
sporty
trendy

shoelaces

leather

hiking boots   athletic shoes   slippers   shoes

Talking and thinking

Let's have a talk
chat
conversation
discussion
gossip
heart-to-heart

Please talk quietly
keep your voice down
talk softly
whisper

Don't talk so loudly
bellow
holler
raise your voice
shout
yell

I think it's too late
believe
expect
feel
guess
imagine
reckon
suppose

Let's think about what to do
chew over
concentrate on
consider
contemplate
decide
focus on
weigh up
work out

I think you're wrong
believe
consider
reckon

We must think up a plan
come up with
create
dream up
invent

Amy likes to sit and think
brood
dream
imagine
ponder
reflect
wonder

Other words for 'say'...

announce
declare
state

answer
reply
respond

ask
beg
demand
inquire
question

mention
comment
point out

mutter
mumble
murmur

Action words

walk
hike
march
plod
saunter
stagger
stomp
stride
stroll
trek
trudge
wander

climb
clamber
scale
scramble

jump
bound
hurdle
leap
spring

push
drive
force
press
prod
ram
shove

pull
drag
heave
tow
tug
yank

take
grab
help yourself
pick
seize
select
snatch

give
deliver
hand over
pass
present

hold
clasp
cling on to
clutch
grab
grasp
grip
hang on to
seize

carry
lift
lug
move
shift
transport

put
dump
lay
leave
place
plunk
rest
set
stand

squash
crumple
crush
flatten
squeeze

sit
perch
rest
sprawl
squat

run

race

dash

sprint

gallop

hurtle

15

All sorts of feelings

I'm feeling ...

weary

energetic

delighted

uneasy

proud

angry
cross
fuming
furious
irate
livid
seething

bored
fed-up
restless

confused
baffled
bewildered
dazed
flummoxed
mixed-up
puzzled

surprised
amazed
astonished
shocked
startled
stunned

happy
cheerful
chirpy
glad
overjoyed
over the moon

excited
eager
keen
thrilled
wound up

worried
anxious
distressed
fretful
on edge
tense
troubled

sad
depressed
devastated
down in the
   dumps
heartbroken
low
miserable
tearful
unhappy
wretched

contented

nervous

confident

flustered

Love and hate

I love ...
adore
am devoted to
am in love with
am very fond of
think the world of

I hate ...
can't bear
can't stand
despise
detest
loathe

tired
exhausted
shattered
sleepy
worn out

grumpy
annoyed
bad-tempered
cranky
cross
grouchy
irritable
peeved

upset
distressed
hurt
shaken

scared
afraid
frightened
panic-stricken
petrified
scared stiff
startled
terrified

**When you're
angry, you ...**
clench your fists
grind your teeth
scream
shout
slam doors
stomp your foot
yell

**When you're
sad, you cry**
burst into floods
of tears
shed tears
snivel
sob
wail
weep
whimper

**When you're happy,
you smile**
beam
grin
grin from ear
to ear
smirk

All kinds of people

People can be ...

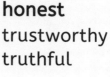

young
babyish
childish
youthful

old
aged
ancient
elderly

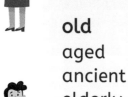

strong
athletic
hefty
muscular
strapping

weak
delicate
feeble
helpless
puny

healthy
fine
fit
in good shape
well

cheerful
cheery
chipper
happy
jolly
light-hearted
optimistic

calm
easy-going
laid-back
peaceful
relaxed

nervous
jittery
jumpy
on edge
tense

crazy
foolish
idiotic
insane
loony
silly

honest
trustworthy
truthful

dishonest
deceitful
two-faced

polite
courteous
well behaved

rude
bad-mannered
brazen
impolite

unkind
cruel
mean
nasty
spiteful

kind
caring
generous
helpful
warm-hearted

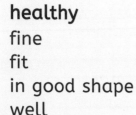
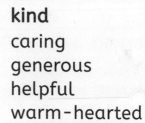

brave
bold
courageous
daring
fearless
plucky

clever
brainy
bright
gifted
intelligent
knowledgeable
smart
talented
wise

clumsy
awkward
bumbling
butter-fingered

funny
amusing
comical
hilarious
ridiculous
witty

picky
choosy
fussy
hard-to-please
particular

lively
bouncy
bubbly
chatty
confident
energetic
full of life
high-spirited

naughty
badly behaved
contrary
disobedient
mischievous
wild

nosy
curious
inquisitive
interfering
prying
snooping

proud
arrogant
boastful
conceited
haughty
high and mighty
snobbish
snooty
stuck-up
uppity
vain

sensible
down-to-earth
level-headed
practical
wise

shy
bashful
quiet
self-conscious
timid

confident
calm
fearless
poised

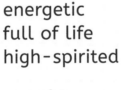
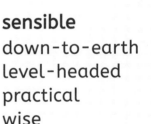

Your body

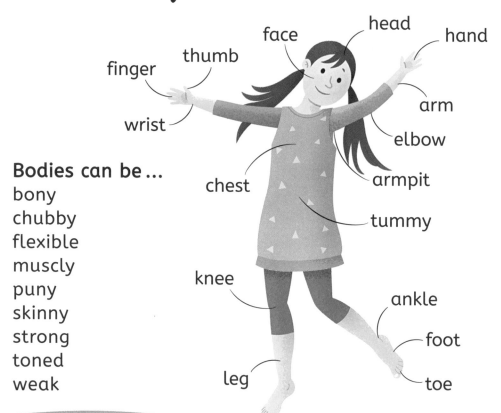

face head hand

finger thumb

wrist arm

elbow

chest armpit

tummy

Bodies can be...
bony
chubby
flexible
muscly
puny
skinny
strong
toned
weak

knee ankle

foot

leg toe

Inside your body

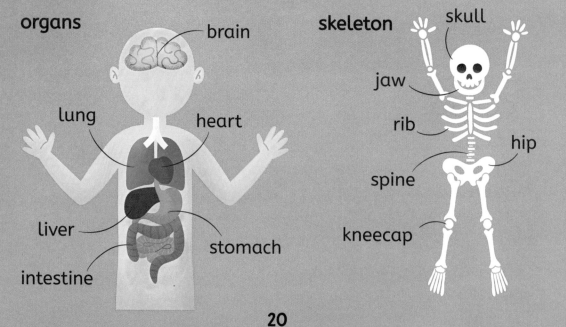

organs

brain

lung heart

liver stomach

intestine

skeleton

skull

jaw

rib

hip

spine

kneecap

Your senses

I can smell roses.
scent
sense
sniff out
track down

Smell this perfume.
breathe in
inhale
sniff

Taste this treat.
nibble
sample
sip
try

Can you taste lime in this dish?
make out
notice
recognize

chirp chirp!

Did you hear that noise?
catch
notice
pick up

Please listen!
concentrate
pay attention
prick up your ears
take in

Did you see that star?
catch sight of
notice
spot

Please don't look.
gaze
peek
peer
watch

You won't feel any pain.
be aware of
experience
notice

Feel this scarf.
handle
run your hands over
touch

Feeling sick

I've got a ...

bruise

cut

headache

lump

rash

stomachache

temperature

toothache

Are you ...?

coughing

shivering

atishoo!

sneezing

itching

I'm feeling ...
awful
bad
faint
poorly
shaky
sick
unwell

You could have ...
an allergy
a broken bone
a bug
a cold
a disease
an infection
a virus

Or you could have ...
asthma
chickenpox
hay fever
flu
pinkeye
strep throat

22

Getting better

Hospital words
accident and
   emergency
clinic
operating room
wing

You may need ...
an appointment
an examination
an operation
a prescription
a shot
an x-ray

ambulance

attendant

wheelchair

crutches

nurse

cast

sling

stethoscope

doctor

In a medicine cabinet ...

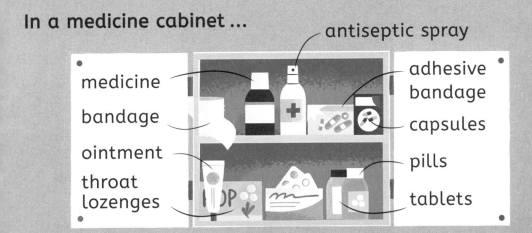

antiseptic spray

medicine

adhesive
bandage

bandage

capsules

ointment

pills

throat
lozenges

tablets

We need to take
   care of Jess.

care for
cure
look after
nurse

Then she'll
   get better.

get well
heal
improve
recover

Now she's
   feeling fine.

all right
better
fit
healthy

Food and drinks

Food can taste ...
bitter
bland
fresh
moldy
rich
salty
sour
stale
sweet

Food can feel ...
chewy
creamy
greasy
juicy
lumpy
rubbery
slimy
stringy

soft
gooey
mushy
sloppy
soggy
spongy
squishy

hard
crisp
crunchy
tough

Fruit
apple
cherries
grapes
lemon
lime
peach
strawberries

melon   pineapple
pear
grapes
orange
plum   bunch of bananas

Fish
catfish
cod
haddock
salmon
sardines
tilapia
tuna

Seafood
clams
crab
lobster
mussels
oysters
scallops
shrimp

FISH FILLETS

SHELLFISH

Meat
bacon
buffalo
chicken
goose

pork
ham
kidney
lamb

liver
salami
steak
turkey

PORK CHOPS

CHICKEN DRUMSTICKS

SPICY SAUSAGES

GROUND BEEF

In a salad you may find ...
avocado
celery
cucumber
green onions
lettuce
olives
peppers
tomatoes

Vegetables
beans
cabbage
cauliflower
eggplant
mushrooms
peas
spinach
squash
string beans

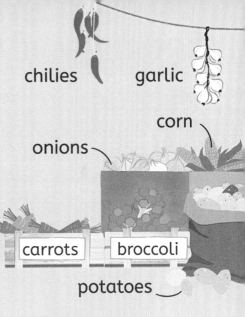

chilies
garlic
corn
onions
carrots
broccoli
potatoes

Takeout food
burger
fries
ice cream
noodles
pasta
pizza
sandwich
tacos

Bread and cakes
bagel
biscuit
bread roll
brownie
bun
cupcake
doughnut
muffin
pancake
pita

SLICED LOAF

Dairy foods
butter
cheese
cottage cheese
cream cheese
goat's cheese
margarine
milk
sour cream
yogurt

MILK

Drinks
coffee
juice
lemonade
milk shake
smoothie
soda
tea
water

Drinks can be ...
fizzy
sparkling

refreshing
thirst-quenching

warm
lukewarm
tepid

cold
chilled
freezing cold
ice-cold

hot
boiling hot
piping hot
scalding

Eating and drinking

eat
bite
chew
gnaw
gobble
munch
nibble

drink
gulp
slurp
suck

You eat quickly
fast
hurriedly
rapidly
swiftly

I eat slowly
carefully
steadily

Food can be ...
delicious
mouthwatering
scrumptious
tasty
yummy

disgusting
foul
revolting
vile

pitcher

I'm thirsty

I'm hungry

Yuck!

glass

fork

knife

plate

spoon

mug

cup

mustard

ketchup

pie dish

How much food?

a crumb

a bite

a slice

a spoonful

a bowlful

a piece

a plateful

In the kitchen

grater

scales

vent

saucepan

strainer colander ladle toaster

frying pan

refrigerator

sink

freezer

spatula

apron

mixing bowl

recipe

cutter

blender

rolling pin

cutting board

whisk

casserole dish

wooden spoon

baking tray

Ways to prepare food

beat	stir
blend	whip
grate	
knead	**chop**
mash	cut up
mix	dice
peel	slice

Ways to cook food

bake	poach
barbecue	roast
boil	simmer
deep-fry	steam
fry	stew
grill	stir-fry
microwave	toast

Inside a home

tiled roof

chimney

attic/loft

drainpipe

bedside table

bedroom

double bed

bathroom

shower

staircase/ stairs

sitting room/living room/lounge

study

desk

balcony

garage

kitchen

dining room

front door

In the kitchen
blender
cabinet
dishwasher
kettle
microwave oven
mixer
oven
sink
stove
toaster

On the floor
carpet
floorboards
tiles
rugs

On the walls
paint
tiles
wallpaper

Types of furniture
armchair
bookcase
bunk bed
chest of drawers
dining table
dresser
rocking chair
single bed
sofa/couch

28

Homes and gardens

Homes can feel
airy
cozy
cramped
damp
dark
drafty
dusty
homely
luxurious
roomy
spacious
stuffy
welcoming

This house is ...

messy
cluttered
untidy

neat
tidy
well-organized

clean
immaculate
polished
scrubbed
spick-and-span

Different homes
apartment
condo
cottage
farmhouse
houseboat
loft
log cabin
mansion
mobile home
palace
ranch
split level house

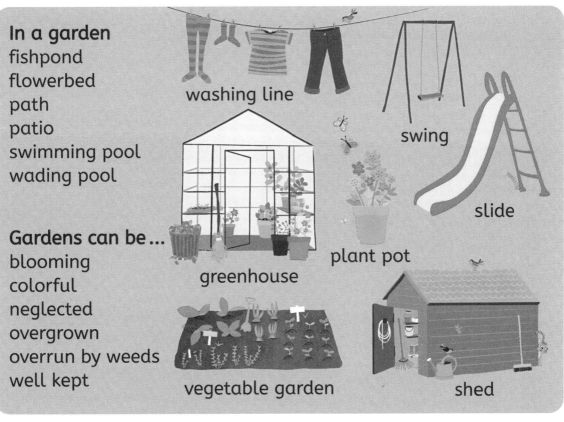

In a garden
fishpond
flowerbed
path
patio
swimming pool
wading pool

washing line

swing

slide

plant pot

Gardens can be ...
blooming
colorful
neglected
overgrown
overrun by weeds
well kept

greenhouse

vegetable garden

shed

Building words

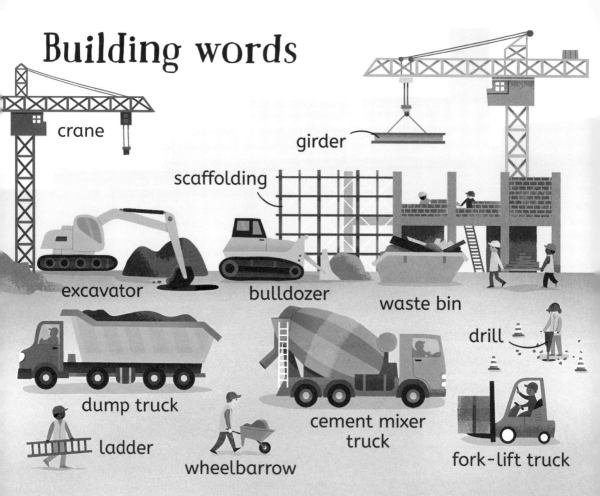

crane

girder

scaffolding

excavator

bulldozer

waste bin

drill

dump truck

ladder

wheelbarrow

cement mixer truck

fork-lift truck

build
construct
erect
put up

People on site
architect
builder
electrician
laborer
plasterer
plumber
site manager

Vehicles and machinery
excavator
front loader
pneumatic drill
rock breaker

Buildings can be made from...
brick
concrete
steel
timber

On a building site you can hear...
banging
crashing
hammering
sawing
shouting
shoveling
thumping

hard hat

cement

trowel

bricklayer

Tools and materials

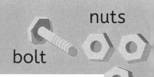

nuts

bolt

Materials can be ...

soft
springy
squashy

hard
firm
rigid
solid
stiff

strong
sturdy
tough

weak
brittle
flimsy
fragile

clear
see-through
transparent

smooth
glossy
polished
silky
sleek

Different materials
glass
leather
metal
paper
plastic
rubber
stone
wood

Types of metal
aluminum
brass
bronze
copper
gold
iron
lead
silver
steel
tin

Types of wood
ash
beech
cedar
ebony
mahogany
oak
pine

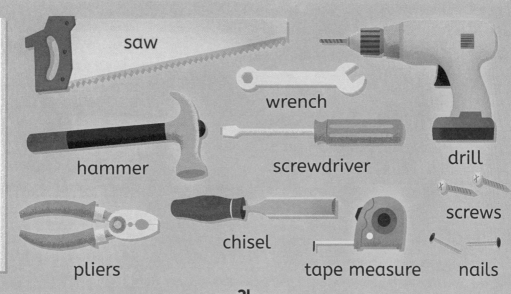

spirit level

saw

wrench

hammer

screwdriver

drill

screws

pliers

chisel

tape measure

nails

In a city

Cities can be ...

busy
bustling
buzzing
crowded
exciting
lively
noisy
packed

dirty
grimy
polluted
smoggy
smoky

empty
deserted
echoing
eerie

shabby
run-down
scruffy

shiny
gleaming
glittering
sparkling

hotel

cathedral

high-rise apartments

library

theater

movie theater

restaurant

coffee shop

shopper

commuter

entertainer

window cleaner

office building

billboard

City buildings can be ...
futuristic
grand
imposing
impressive
stunning

shopping center

mosque

college

flower stand

art gallery

museum

bank

road sweeper

subway

human statue

tourist

newspaper seller

tour guide

33

Going shopping

market   barber   bookstore   pet store   florist

toy store   boutique   butcher shop   newsagent

cash machine

bank   salon   post office   shoe store   bakery

store
department store
superstore

cheap
inexpensive
reasonable
reduced

money
cash
change
payment

card   coins

bill

At a supermarket

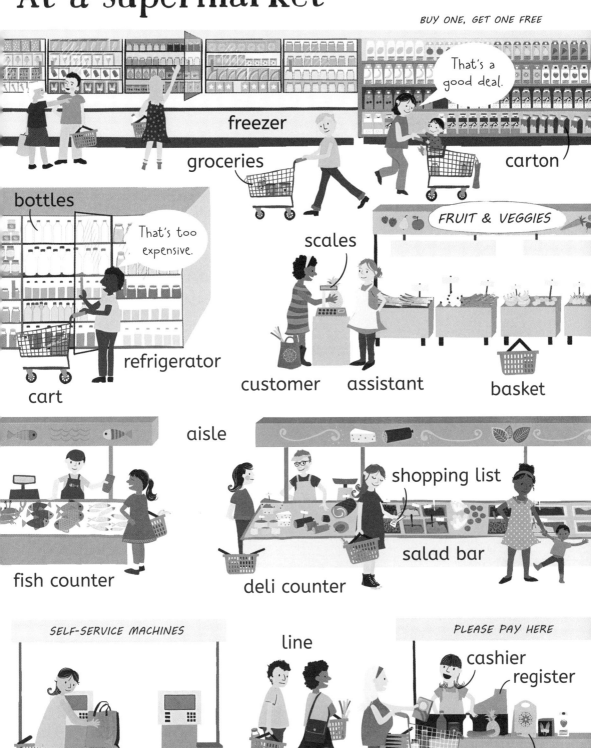

BUY ONE, GET ONE FREE

That's a good deal.

freezer

groceries

carton

bottles

That's too expensive.

scales

FRUIT & VEGGIES

refrigerator

cart

customer   assistant

basket

aisle

shopping list

salad bar

fish counter

deli counter

SELF-SERVICE MACHINES

line

PLEASE PAY HERE

cashier

register

reusable bag

checkout

grocery bag

35

On the road

Vehicles may ...
accelerate
brake
break down
collide
crash
crawl
cruise
race
skid
slow down
speed up
squeal to a halt
swerve
veer

toot!

bus

bus stop

zoom!

hon

sports car

motorhome

pedestrian crossing

traffic circle

road sign

camper van

fire engine

Cars can be ...
dented
gleaming
rusty
streamlined

steering wheel

windshield

hood

trunk

headlight

tire

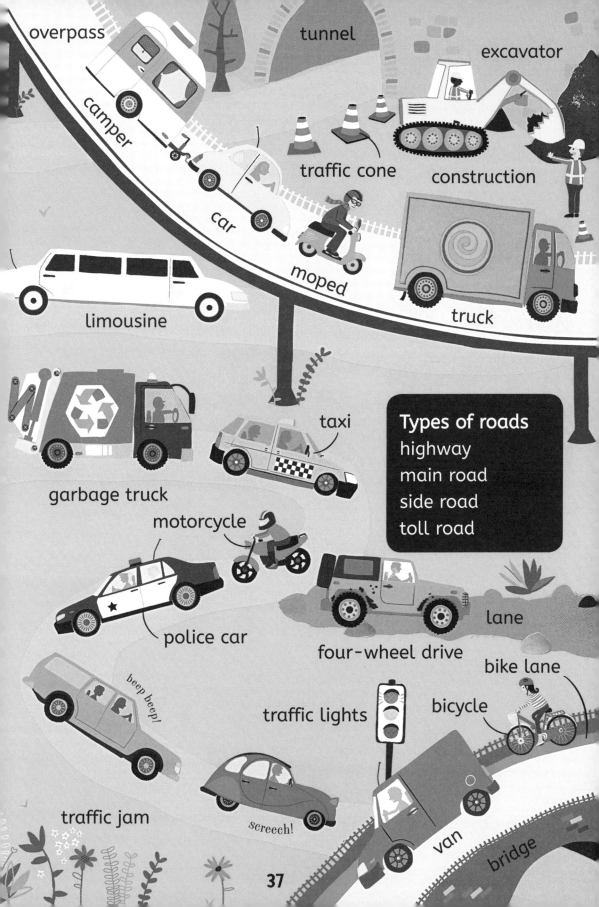

overpass

tunnel

excavator

camper

traffic cone

construction

car

moped

truck

limousine

garbage truck

taxi

Types of roads
highway
main road
side road
toll road

motorcycle

police car

four-wheel drive

lane

bike lane

traffic lights

bicycle

beep beep!

traffic jam

screech!

van

bridge

37

Ships and boats

bow (front)

container

funnel

stern (back)

anchor

container ship

hull

Land ahoy!

canoe

icebreaker

sail

engine

life jacket

paddle

motorboat

kayak

sailboat

Ships and boats may ...
bob up and
   down
capsize
cruise
dock
drift
float

moor
plow through
   the waves
put to sea
roll
set sail
sink
steam ahead

On board a ship
captain
cooks
crew
engineers
officers
passengers
sailors
stewards

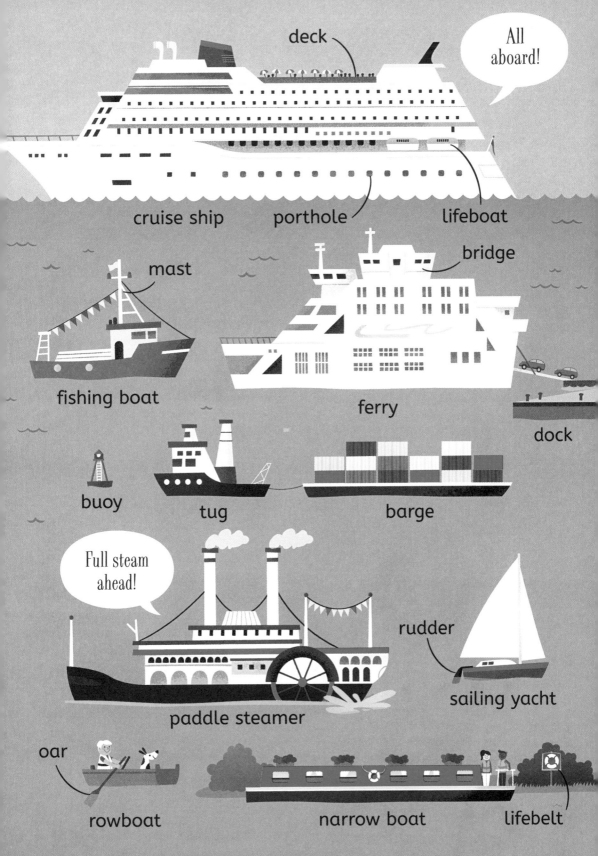

39

Trains, planes and aircraft

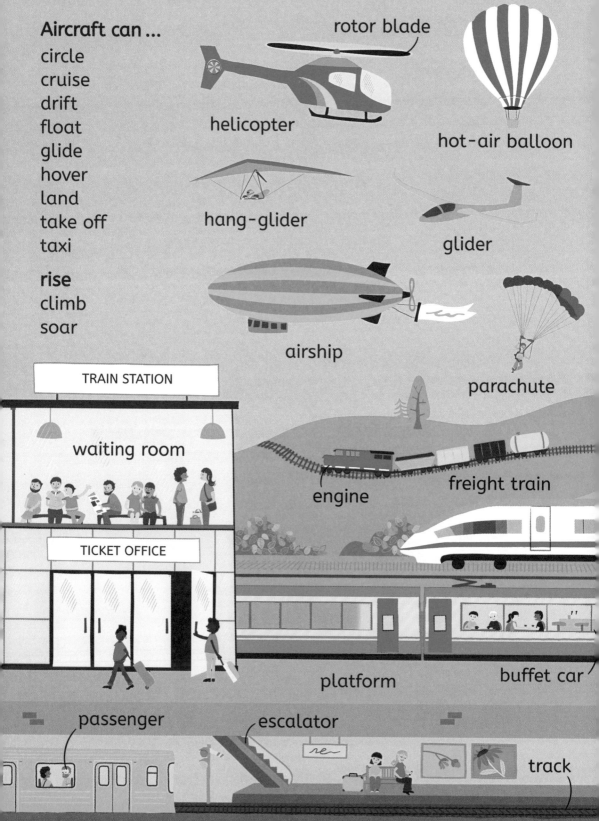

Aircraft can ...
circle
cruise
drift
float
glide
hover
land
take off
taxi

rise
climb
soar

rotor blade

helicopter

hot-air balloon

hang-glider

glider

airship

parachute

TRAIN STATION

waiting room

TICKET OFFICE

engine

freight train

platform

buffet car

passenger

escalator

track

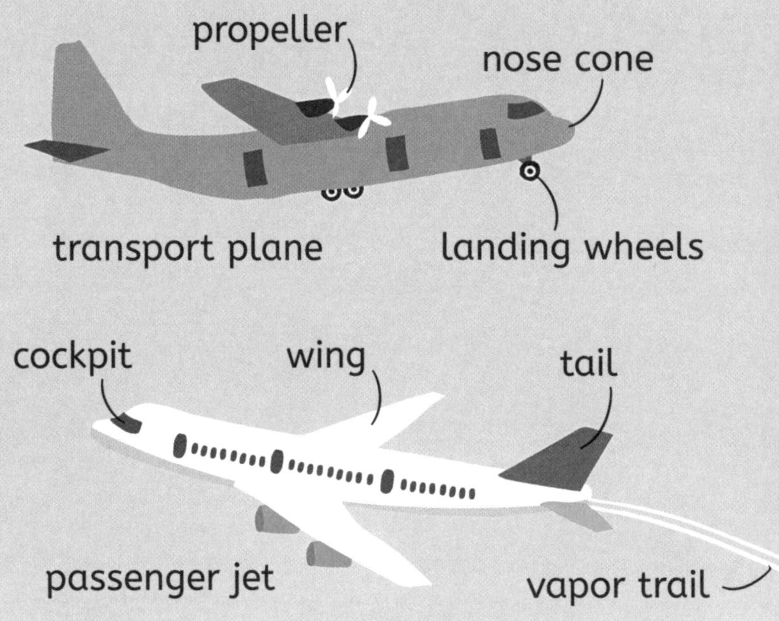

propeller

nose cone

Inside a plane
aisle
cabin
food cart
in-flight
  entertainment
life jacket
oxygen mask
seat belt
sick bag

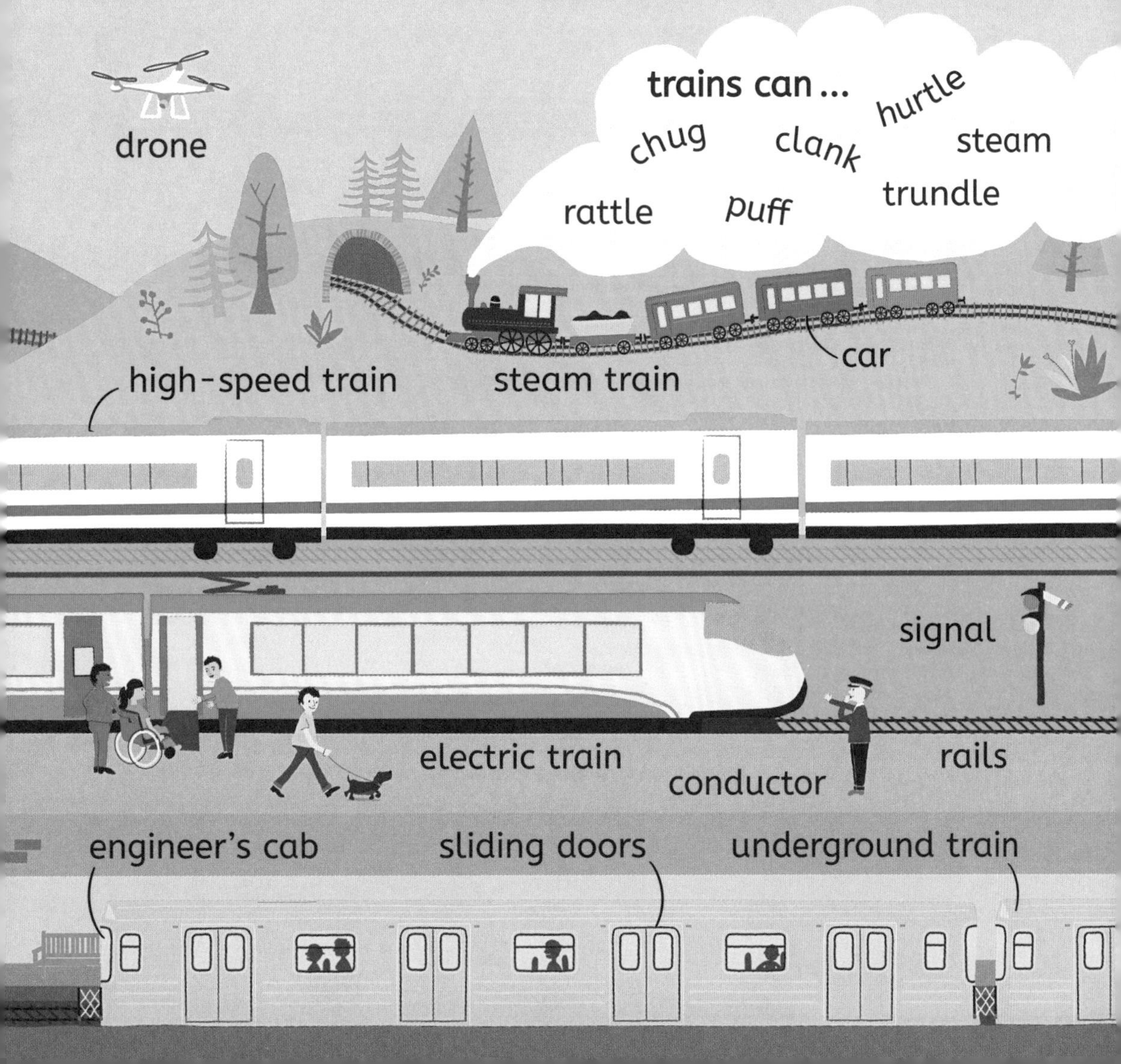

transport plane

landing wheels

cockpit   wing   tail

passenger jet

vapor trail

drone

trains can ...
chug   clank   hurtle   steam
rattle   puff   trundle

high-speed train   steam train

car

signal

electric train

conductor   rails

engineer's cab   sliding doors   underground train

At an airport

We're going
   on a ...
flight
journey
trip

vacation
getaway

We may feel ...
excited
fidgety
tired
travel-sick

Flights can be ...
canceled
delayed
on time
rescheduled

When do we ...
leave?
depart
set off
take off

arrive?
land
reach our
   destination
touch down

airplane

hangar

baggage cart

shuttle bus

laptop bag

backpack

wheeled luggage

hand luggage

SECURITY

X-ray
machine

security
guard

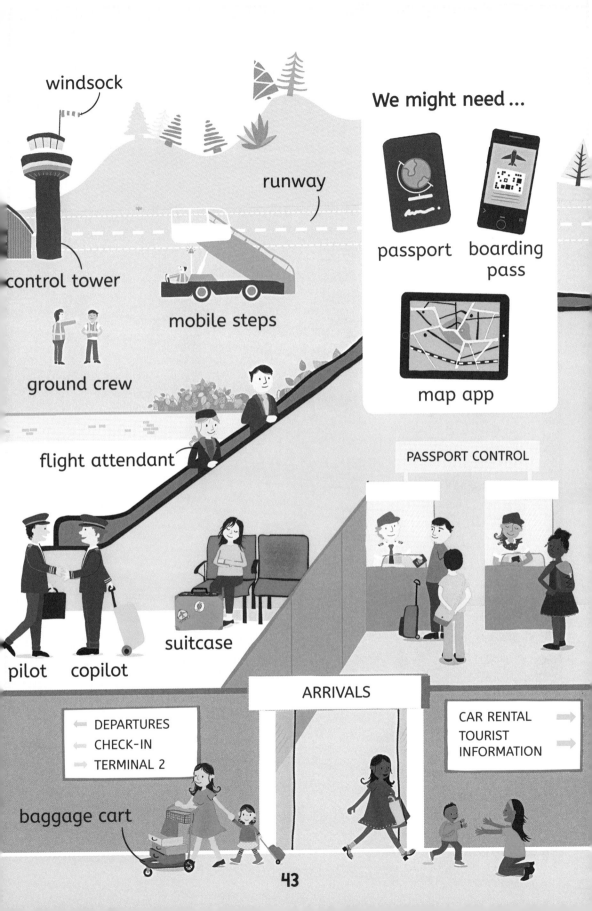

windsock

runway

control tower

mobile steps

ground crew

We might need ...

passport

boarding pass

map app

flight attendant

PASSPORT CONTROL

pilot copilot

suitcase

ARRIVALS

← DEPARTURES
← CHECK-IN
⇒ TERMINAL 2

CAR RENTAL ⇒
TOURIST
INFORMATION ⇒

baggage cart

Jobs people do

job
career
work

boss
director
manager
supervisor

Jobs can be ...
difficult
easy
enjoyable
exciting
fun
hard
interesting
rewarding
satisfying
tiring

All sorts of jobs
accountant
architect
builder
designer
doctor
electrician
engineer
farmer
journalist
lawyer
librarian
musician
nurse
painter
pharmacist
social worker
teacher

dentist

decorator

chef

police officer

plumber

gardener

vet

zookeeper

waiter

carpenter

hairdresser

receptionist

mechanic

scientist

artist

firefighter

Fun and hobbies

We like to have fun
enjoy ourselves
have a good time

fun
enjoyment
entertainment
pleasure

Hobbies and interests
ballet
chess
computer games
cooking
dancing
drawing
fishing
judo
karate
painting
photography
reading
rollerblading
skateboarding
swimming

Art equipment
acrylic paints
canvas
chalk
crayons
easel
eraser
felt-tip markers
paintbrush
paints
pastels
pencil
watercolors

Things to read
atlas
comic
graphic novel
magazine
novel
picture book
reference book
storybook

Types of stories
adventure story
detective story
fairy tale
ghost story
mystery
science fiction
  story

Types of computers
games console
laptop
tablet
PC

Computer games can be ...
amazing
educational
exciting
frustrating
fun
gripping
realistic
superrealistic
time-consuming
violent

easy
basic
simple
straightforward

hard
advanced
challenging
complex
complicated
difficult
testing

Dance and theater

Some types of dance
disco dancing
folk dancing
jazz dancing
salsa
tango

line dancing

Dancers ...
glide
leap
pirouette
spin
stomp
strut
sway
twirl

Dancers may be ...
dainty
elegant
flexible
graceful
sprightly

tutu

ballerina

ballet

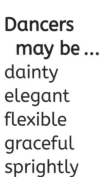

street dancing

tap-dancing

ballroom dancing

At a theater you can see a ...
ballet
comedy show
concert
dance performance
musical
pantomime
play
puppet show
talent show

Theater words
actor
cast
chorus
costume
director
intermission
makeup
rehearsal
scene
script
stage manager

On a set
lighting
props
scenery

In a theater
aisle
balcony
box
curtain
seats
stage

Movies and TV

Movies can be ...

exciting
action-packed
fast-moving
gripping
nail-biting

boring
dull
uninteresting
slow-moving
tedious

funny
comical
hilarious
ridiculous
side-splitting
whacky

sad
depressing
moving
tear-jerking
tragic

frightening
creepy
hair-raising
scary
spine-chilling
spooky
terrifying

WOW!

SHHHH!

AARGH!

HA HA HA!

Movies and TV programs
cartoon
talk show
comedy
detective series
documentary
drama
game show
horror movie
news
science fiction

Movies may include ...
animation
close-up shots
computer
   graphics
flashbacks
slow-motion
   shots
sound effects
special effects
surround sound

In a movie theater, you may hear ...
coughing
crunching
gasping
giggling
laughing
munching
rustling
slurping
sobbing
whispering

At a fair

roller coaster

ferris wheel

haunted train

big slide

carousel

fair
amusement park
funfair
theme park

Fairground amusements
bouncy castle
bumper cars
hall of mirrors
merry-go-round
roller coaster
simulator
swingboats
teacup ride

Rides can be ...
exciting
fast
gentle
nail-biting
scary
thrilling

On a ride you may ...
bounce
lurch
plunge
spin
whirl

Fair lights can be ...
blazing
colorful
dazzling
flashing
magical

Fair music can be ...
blaring
booming
deafening
pounding
thumping

At a circus

tightrope walker

trapeze artists

audience

clown

strongman

ringmaster

acrobats

eek!

Circus performers may ...
balance on a tightrope
bounce on a trampoline
fly through the air
juggle
ride a unicycle
spin plates
swallow fire
take a bow
walk on stilts
walk on their hands

Acrobats do ...
backflips
backward rolls
forward rolls
handstands
leaps
somersaults
tumbles
twists

Clowns may ...
do slapstick routines
mime
throw custard pies

The audience may ...
cover their eyes
gape
gasp

applaud
cheer
clap

laugh
cackle
chortle
chuckle
giggle
roar with laughter

Music words

Music words
beat
harmony
melody
rhythm
tune

stave

bass clef

treble clef

song
number
track
tune

Types of music
classical
country
folk
hip-hop
jazz
pop
rap
reggae
rock

quarter

notes

2 eighth
notes

I play in a ...
band
group
orchestra

keyboard

squeak!

parp!

trumpet

bow

violin

tootle!

clarinet

stage

Music may sound...

lively
dramatic
exciting
thrilling

calm
peaceful
soothing

Musicians may ...

perform
play
practice
rehearse

clash! *crash!*

drum kit

percussion instruments

xylophone

triangle

maracas

cymbals

Singers may ...

chant
hum
screech
trill
warble

strum! *twang!*

guitar

parp!

saxophone

58

microphone

lead singer

More musical instruments

accordion
cello
double bass
electric guitar
flute
harp
organ
piano
recorder
tambourine
trombone

baton

music stand

Musical equipment

amplifier
speakers
synthesizer

score

conductor

All sorts of sports

Types of sports
athletics
badminton
boxing
cross country
fencing
football golf
gymnastics
hockey
ice hockey
judo
netball
rowing
rugby
show jumping
skating
table tennis
taekwondo
wrestling

skateboarding

baseball

wetsuit

surfing

bow

wicket

arrow

archery

cricket

volleyball

karate

Athletics events	Sports places	Athletes must be ...
decathlon	arena	athletic
discus	court	determined
high jump	dome	energetic
hurdles	field	fit
javelin	ring	in great shape
long jump	rink	muscular
pentathlon	sports hall	skillful
pole vault	stadium	speedy
sprint	track	strong

mask

fencing

hoop

basketball

gymnastics

swimming

cycling

tennis

soccer

Types of sporting event
challenge
competition
contest
cross-country run
final
game
heat
marathon
match
Olympics
Paralympics
qualifying round
quarterfinal
race
replay
semifinal
time trial
tournament

Sports moves

kick	**hit**	**throw**	**dodge**
dribble	drive	bowl	duck
pass	knock	chuck	sidestep
	putt	fling	swerve
catch	slam	hurl	
grab	strike	pass	
grasp	swipe at	pitch	
snatch	volley	toss	
seize	whack		

medal

trophy

Cats and dogs

Cats can be ...
curious
independent
sleek
snuggly
timid

kitten

meow
cry
mew

purr!

Cats may ...
yowl

hiss

scratch

slink

collar

leash

yelp!

dalmatian

labrador

woof!

greyhound

poodle

dachshund

puppy

Dogs can be ...
affectionate
gentle
loyal
lively
bouncy
playful

obedient
well trained

disobedient
mischievous
naughty
wild

Dogs may ...
bark
growl
wag their
tails
whine

More pets

Pets may ...
creep
flutter
slither

bite
chew
gnaw
munch
nibble
nip

jump
leap
pounce
spring

run
scamper
scurry
scuttle
trot

hiss!

snake

tweet!

parakeet

wheel

hamster

snuffle!

rabbit

gerbil

squeak!

mouse

tank

chameleon

guinea pig

tropical fish

Pets can look ...

scaly

furry

fluffy

wiry

Horses and riding

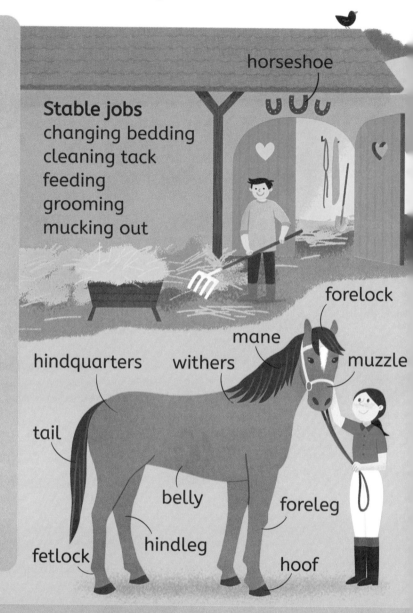

Horses may ...
bolt
buck
canter
gallop
graze
jump
kick
nuzzle
plod
prance
rear
shy
stride
trot
walk

Horse noises
clip-clop
neigh
snort
whicker
whinny

Stable jobs
changing bedding
cleaning tack
feeding
grooming
mucking out

horseshoe

forelock

mane

muzzle

hindquarters   withers

tail

belly

foreleg

hindleg

fetlock

hoof

Horses may be ...	or they may be ...	horse
calm	frisky	colt (young male)
gentle	highly strung	filly (young female)
good-natured	nervous	foal (baby horse)
obedient	skittish	mare (female)
surefooted	stubborn	pony (small horse)
well trained	wild	stallion (male)

horse trailer

jump

curry comb

bridle

riding hat

reins

pony

saddle

bit

stirrup

jodhpurs

riding boots

Horses eat ...
apples
carrots
hay
linseed cake
mash
oats
pony nuts

Riding equipment
crop
harness
leading rein
stable blanket

Riding events
cross-country
dressage
flat racing
hacking
hurdling
point-to-point
pony games
pony trekking
showjumping

Types of horses
carthorse
hunter
polo pony
racehorse
show-jumper
thoroughbred

Horses can look ...
dainty
elegant
glossy
shaggy
sleek
stocky

Horse colors
bay
chestnut
dapple-gray
gray
palomino
piebald

Bugs and insects

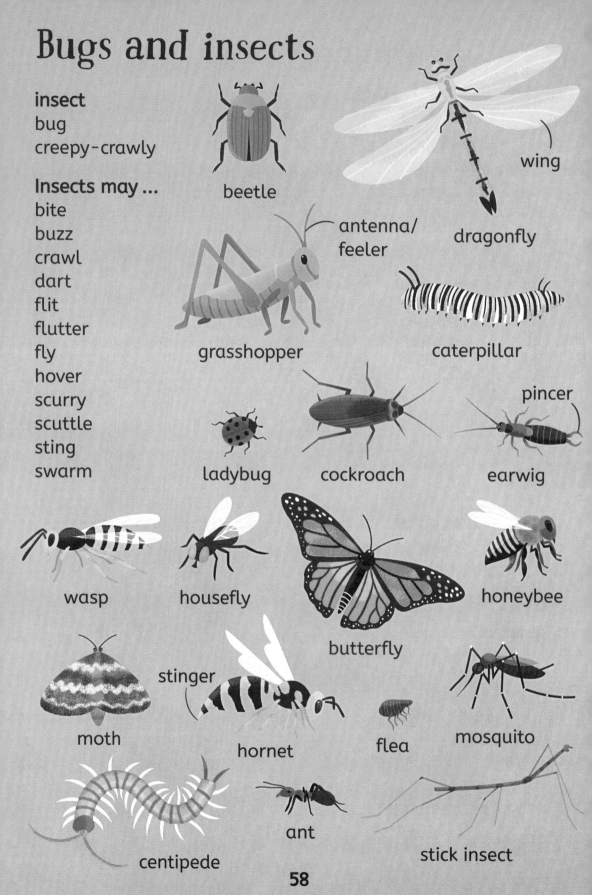

insect
bug
creepy-crawly

Insects may ...
bite
buzz
crawl
dart
flit
flutter
fly
hover
scurry
scuttle
sting
swarm

beetle

wing

dragonfly

antenna/
feeler

grasshopper

caterpillar

pincer

ladybug

cockroach

earwig

wasp

housefly

honeybee

butterfly

stinger

moth

hornet

flea

mosquito

centipede

ant

stick insect

58

Animal words

Some types of animals

mammal

bird

amphibian

insect

reptile

fish

animal
creature
beast

Animal habitats
desert
grassland
mountain
swamp
woodland

Animal sounds
bark
hiss
howl
quack
roar
screech
squawk
squeal

Animal groups
a flock of sheep
a herd of cows
a litter of puppies
a pack of wolves
a pod of whales
a pride of lions
a school of fish
a swarm of bees

Males, females and babies

animal	male	female	baby
chicken →	rooster →	hen →	chick
cow →	bull →	cow →	calf
horse →	stallion →	mare →	foal
pig →	boar →	sow →	piglet
sheep →	ram →	ewe →	lamb

Bird words

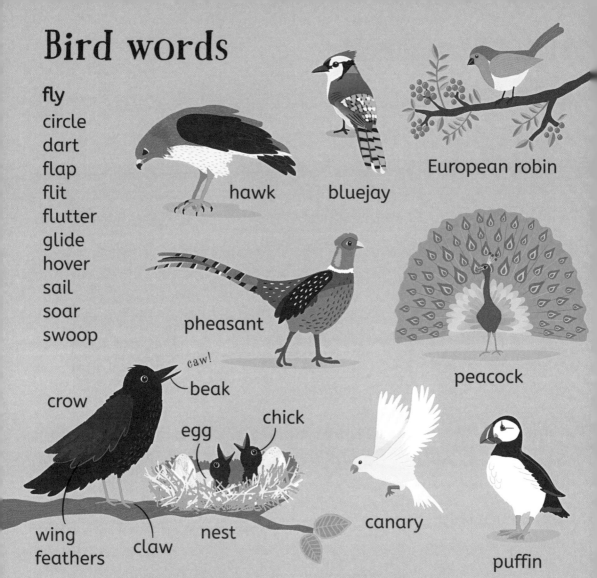

fly
circle
dart
flap
flit
flutter
glide
hover
sail
soar
swoop

hawk

bluejay

European robin

pheasant

peacock

crow

caw!

beak

egg

chick

wing
feathers

claw

nest

canary

puffin

More types of birds

		Bird noises	
bullfinch	lark	cackle	honk
cuckoo	magpie	call	hoot
dove	nightingale	chatter	pipe
emu	ostrich	cheep	quack
falcon	raven	chirp	screech
goose	sparrow	chirrup	sing
heron	stork	cluck	squawk
jackdaw	swallow	coo	trill
kingfisher	thrush	gobble	tweet
kookaburra	woodpecker	hiss	twitter

coo coo!

pigeon

hummingbird

screech!

blackbird

seagull

HOOT!

pelican

owl

eagle

flamingo

quack!

duck

bird of paradise

Birds may ...
dive
hop
paddle
peck
perch
plummet
pounce
roost
strut
waddle

A bird's feathers can look ...
bedraggled
fluffy
ruffled
shiny
smooth

downy

glossy

colorful

speckled

Trees

acorn

conker

Trees can be...
magnificent
spindly
spreading
sturdy

Tree bark can be...
gnarled
papery
ridged
rough
smooth

Types of trees
ash
aspen
beech
birch
buckeye
dogwood
elm
hawthorn
hazel
magnolia
maple
monkey puzzle

oak
olive
palm
poplar
rowan
rubber
sweet chestnut
sweetgum
sycamore
walnut
weeping willow
yew

Evergreen trees

branch

cone

pine   spruce   cedar   holly   redwood

Fruit trees

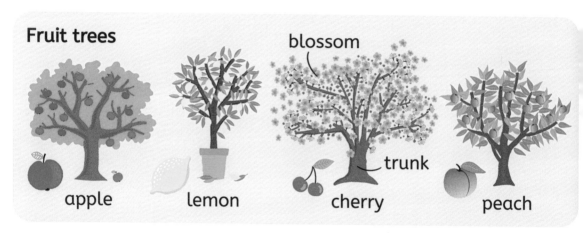

blossom

trunk

apple   lemon   cherry   peach

Bushes and flowers

Types of flowers
carnation
cowslip
daffodil
daisy
dandelion
forget-me-not
gardenia
gerbera
hyacinth
marigold
orchid
primrose
snowdrop
violet
waterlily

Types of bushes
azalea
boxwood
holly
laurel
lavender
lilac
mulberry
rosemary
thyme

Bushes can be ...
bushy
clipped
overgrown
prickly

Flowers can be ...
beautiful
colorful
delicate
spectacular
straggly
sweet-smelling

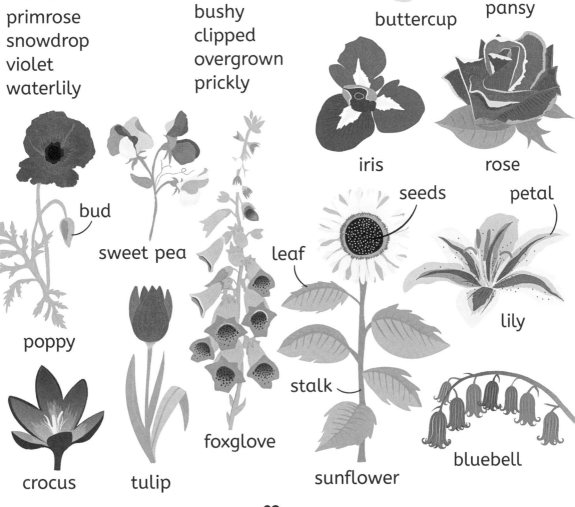

buttercup

pansy

iris

rose

bud

sweet pea

leaf

seeds

petal

poppy

lily

crocus

tulip

foxglove

stalk

sunflower

bluebell

In the country

field
meadow
pasture

path
lane
track
trail

hill
hillside
mound

woods
forest
woodland

Countryside words
barn
cottage
fence
field
gate
grass
hedgerow
lake
pond
pool
scarecrow

In the country you may spot a ...
black bear
mole
opossum
rabbit
raccoon
squirrel

Woods can be ...
dark
filled with
  dappled sunlight
gloomy
shadowy
spooky

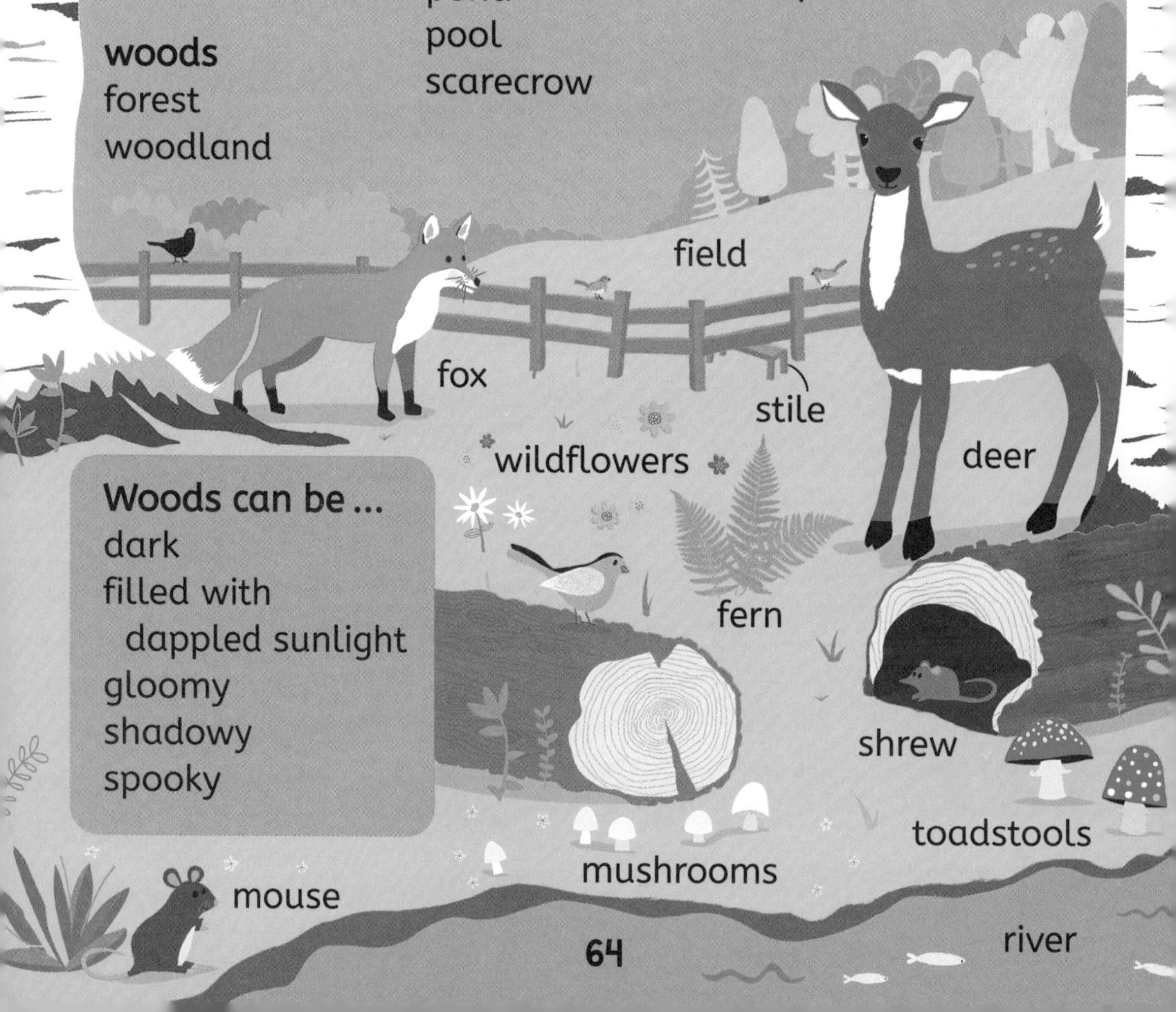

field

fox

stile

wildflowers

deer

fern

shrew

mushrooms

toadstools

mouse

river

On a farm

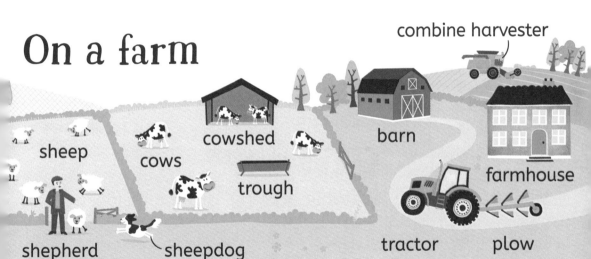

combine harvester

sheep

cows

cowshed

trough

barn

farmhouse

shepherd

sheepdog

tractor

plow

Farmers grow ...
barley
corn
fruit
oats
rice
sugar beet
vegetables
wheat

Some farm animals
donkey
goat
goose
pig

Farm vehicles and machinery
backhoe
baler
cultivator
loader
milking machine
mower
muck-spreader
seed drill
roller
trailer

Farming words
hay
manure
straw

Farming jobs
feeding animals
harvesting crops
herding animals
milking cows
picking fruit
planting vegetables
plowing
rounding up sheep
shearing sheep
sowing seeds
spraying
weeding

henhouse

turkey

duck

rooster

hen

eggs

ducklings

chicks

Rivers, lakes and ponds

river
brook
creek
stream
torrent

Rivers may be ...
choked with weeds
crystal clear
deep
fast-flowing
murky
polluted
shallow
sluggish
sparkling
stagnant

Rivers may ...
babble
break their banks
bubble
burble
cascade
flood
flow
froth
murmur
pour
splash
surge
swirl
trickle
twist
wind

**Along a river
  you might see ...**
delta
dam
gorge (deep valley)
island
weir

**Lake and river
  sports**
fishing
kayaking
sailing
swimming
water-skiing
whitewater
  rafting

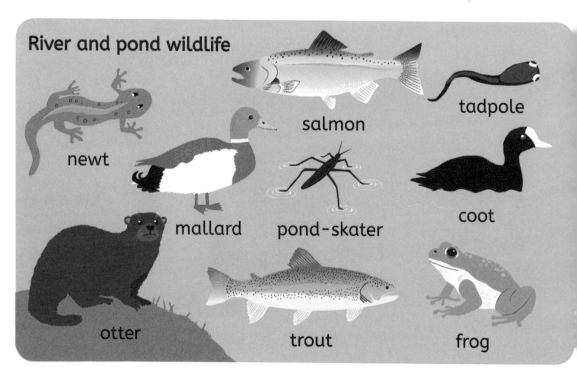

River and pond wildlife

tadpole
salmon
newt
mallard
pond-skater
coot
otter
trout
frog

bridge

rapids

sail boat

lake

dock

river bank

waterfall

stepping stones

mooring dock

rowboat

damselfly

kingfisher

heron

moorhen

toad

pond/pool

reeds

pondweed

frogspawn

waterlily pad

67

In the mountains

Mountains
 can be ...
high
lofty
snow-capped
soaring
towering

Their slopes
 can be ...
craggy
forested
icy
rocky
steep

More mountain
 words
avalanche
black ice
glacier
snowstorm

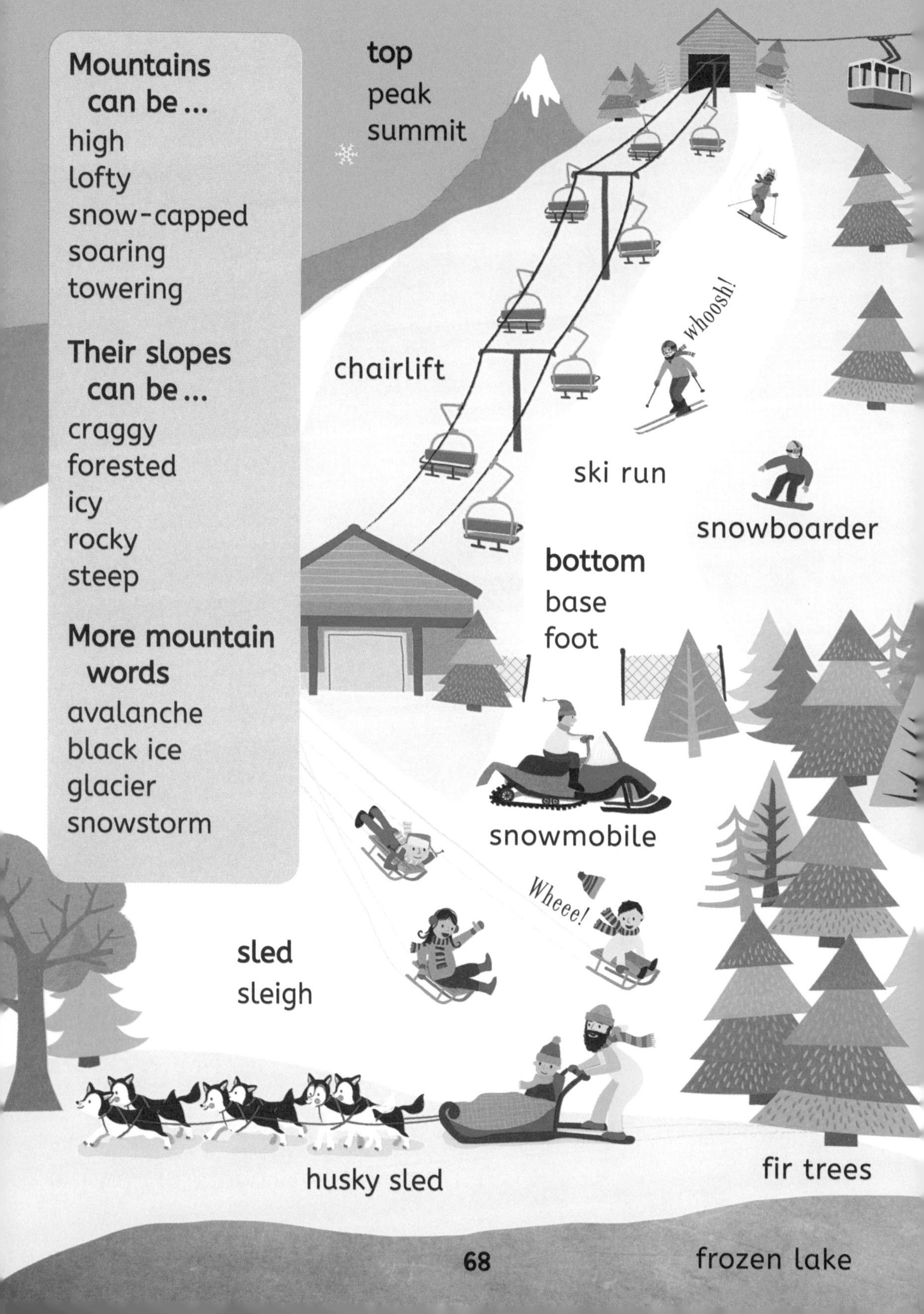

top
peak
summit

chairlift

whoosh!

ski run

snowboarder

bottom
base
foot

snowmobile

Wheee!

sled
sleigh

husky sled

fir trees

68

frozen lake

cable cars

climbing rope

ice ax

slope

slalom course

drag lift
button lift
T-bar

ledge

chalet

bunny slope

SKATE RENTAL

skating rink

cross-country skiers

Mountain sports can be ...
challenging
dangerous
exciting
risky

Climbers ...
clamber
cling onto the rock face
lose their footing
reach the summit
scramble
tumble

Skiers and snowboarders ...
jump
perform tricks
race
speed
swerve

Skaters ...
balance
fall
glide
twirl
wobble

In a desert

palm trees

vulture

camel train

sand dune

oryx

skull

oasis

water hole

cactus

camel

jerboa

cobra

dung beetle

scorpion

Deserts are often...	The sun is...	Some desert animals
dry	blazing	desert fox
sandy	blinding	desert rat
scorching	dazzling	lizard
		locust
but some are...	You may be...	rattlesnake
freezing	parched	tarantula
rocky	sunburned	
stony	sweaty	

In a jungle

canopy
(tree tops)

butterfly

toucan

tree frog

spider monkey

screech!

vine

parrot

sloth

orchid

swamp

jaguar

army ants

Jungles can be...	Jungle trees and plants...	Some jungle animals
dark	coil	armadillo
gloomy	dangle	chimpanzee
humid	loop	gorilla
lush	scratch	orangutan
noisy	snake	python
steamy	sting	tapir
swampy	tower	tiger

Grassland animals

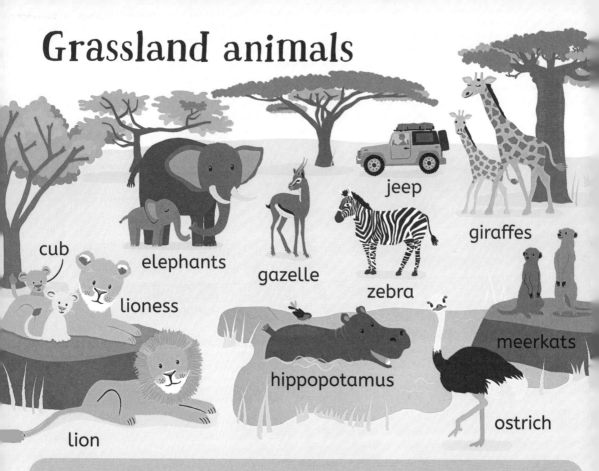

cub

elephants

gazelle

jeep

giraffes

zebra

lioness

meerkats

hippopotamus

ostrich

lion

Animals roam the grasslands ...
plains
savanna

Some grassland animals
antelope
buffalo
cheetah
crocodile
hyena
leopard
rhinoceros
warthog

The animals may ...
attack
charge
hide in the undergrowth
hunt
lie in wait
lurk in the bushes
pounce
prowl
snap their jaws
stalk their prey
thunder over the plain

You may hear a ...
bellow
crash
crunch
growl
grunt
hiss
howl
roar
rustle
screech
snap
snarl
splash
squeal

Under the sea

Fish and sea creatures
dolphin
eel
lobster
porpoise
pufferfish
seahorse
sea lion
sea snake
seal
squid
swordfish
whale

Fish may ...
crest the waves
dart
dive
drift
float
glide
leap out of
 the water
lurk
plunge
splash
surface
swim

Under the sea it can be ...
beautiful
cold
colorful
dark
mysterious
scary
silent

sea
ocean

sea bed
ocean floor

parrotfish

octopus

fin

shark

turtle

school of fish

oxygen tank

mask

scuba diver

clownfish

angelfish

coral reef

ray

At the beach

At the beach you may see...
caves
cliffs
pier
sand dunes
tide pools

A beach resort may be...
crowded
deserted
empty
packed
peaceful
picturesque
quiet
sleepy
touristy

Beaches may be...
pebbly
sandy
stony

Things to take to the beach
beach ball
bucket and shovel
flippers
folding chair
picnic
snorkel
sunglasses
sunscreen
sunhat
swimsuit
towel
wetsuit

Beach activities
building sandcastles
collecting shells
playing mini-golf
sailing
scuba diving
snorkeling
sunbathing
surfing
swimming
wading
water-skiing

Sea words
high tide
low tide
spray
surf
whitecaps

hotel   souvenir shops   ice-cream truck   camper

windbreak   kite   volleyball

surfboard   surfer   pier   kitesurfer

74

Sea and shore

sea
ocean

beach
coast
pebbles
sands
shore

The sea may be ...
calm
choppy
crystal clear
glassy
gray
green
raging
rough
shimmering
sparkling

The waves may ...
billow
break
churn
crash
foam
lap
pound
race
roar
roll
surge
swell

In a tide pool
anemone
barnacle
sea urchin
shrimp

Nature at the beach

driftwood

gull

crab

jellyfish

cormorant

starfish

shells

seaweed

boardwalk

campsite

beach café

lifeguard

umbrella

paddle boat

windsurfer

rubber raft

fishing net

Words for weather

Weather words
climate
temperature
weather forecast

Today, the weather is ...

hot
baking   scorching
blistering   sizzling
boiling   sweltering
roasting   tropical

cold
bitter   freezing
bracing   nippy
chilly   perishing
cool   wintry

cloudy
gloomy
gray
miserable
overcast
dreary
dull

fine
dry
mild
sunny
warm

rainy   **windy**
damp   blowy
drizzly   blustery
showery   breezy
spitting   gusty
wet   stormy

weather vane

foggy   **steamy**
hazy   clammy
misty   close
murky   humid
smoggy   muggy

thermometer

Types of windy weather

breeze   gale   tornado/whirlwind

Types of wet weather

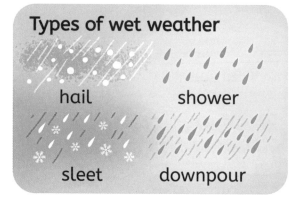

hail   shower

sleet   downpour

Ice, frost and snow

icicle

Snow may...

drift   fall   float   melt   settle   swirl   thaw

Ice can be ...
brittle
cracked
glassy
hard
slippery
smooth

Snow can be ...
crisp
crunchy
dazzling
deep
powdery
slushy

Frost may ...
glisten
glitter
sparkle

**The ground
  may be ...**
as hard as iron
blanketed with
  snow
carpeted with
  snow
dusted with snow
frozen solid
sprinkled with
  snow

**The trees
  may be ...**
bare
covered with
  frost
laden with snow
weighed down
  by snow

In the snow you ...
plod
plow through
sink in
struggle
stumble

On the ice you ...
glide
skate
skid
slide
slip

snowflake

**More ice, frost and
  snow words**
avalanche
Jack Frost
snowball
snowdrift

snowman   sled   snow angel

77

Storm words

storm
blizzard
hurricane
monsoon
snowstorm
thunderstorm
typhoon

Thunder ...
booms
cracks
echoes
growls
roars
rolls
rumbles

Lightning ...
flares
flashes
lights up the sky
strikes
zigzags

Rain ...
beats down
buckets down
lashes down
pelts down
pours down
teems down

Storms can be ...
awesome
deafening
destructive
devastating
dramatic
ear-splitting
frightening
powerful
raging
savage
terrifying
violent
wild

hailstones

forked
lightning

Storms may ...
block roads
bring down
 power lines
cut off towns
damage crops
destroy buildings
flood homes
swell rivers
uproot trees

**More storm
 words**
billowing clouds
inky sky
thunderbolt
thunderclap
thundercloud

The wind ...
howls
gusts
shrieks
rages
blasts
blows

78

Night words

crescent moon

The night may be ...
clear
moonlit
shadowy
starlit

The sky may be ...
inky
pitch-black
starry
velvety

Nighttime sounds
bats sqeaking
cats yowling
clocks chiming
doors slamming
floorboards creaking
owls hooting
people snoring
sirens wailing
windows banging

At night, it can feel ...
ghostly
gloomy
hushed
peaceful
scary
silent
spooky
still

Times of night
dawn
daybreak
dusk
midnight
nightfall
the small hours

Some nighttime animals
fox
hedgehog
skunk

The moon may be ...
bright
hazy
hidden behind a cloud
pale
silvery
waning (growing smaller)
waxing (growing larger)

The stars may ...
flicker
glimmer
glitter
shimmer
shine
sparkle
twinkle

shooting star

owl

fireflies

moths

bat

Fire and fireworks

Fireworks...
blaze
dazzle
explode
fizzle out
flare
shoot
shower
sink
soar
sparkle
spin
spiral
whiz
whoosh
zoom

Fireworks can be...
dazzling
deafening
magical
spectacular
stunning

Firework sounds
boom
splutter
whine
whistle

Types of fireworks
firecracker
fountain
rocket
Roman candle
smoke bombs
sparkler

pop!

crash!

fizz!

hiss!

bang!

crackle!

screech!

squeal!

Fires...
blaze
burn
glow
rage
roar
scorch
smolder

Smoke...
billows
chokes
curls
drifts
envelops
swirls

Flames...
dance
flare
flicker
glow

Noisy words

Stop that noise!
commotion
din
racket
rumpus

Bells ring
chime
clang
jingle
peal

ding-dong!

Doors bang
crash
slam
thud

Children scream
screech
shriek
squeal

Dancers stomp
clatter
clomp
stamp

People shout
bellow
call out
roar
yell

Fountains splash
babble
glug
gurgle

splosh!

Drums boom
roll
thunder
rumble

squeak!

loud	**quiet**	**deep**	**high**
deafening	hushed	booming	high-pitched
ear-splitting	muffled	low	piercing
noisy	soft	low-pitched	shrill

Fairy-tale words

magic
enchantment
sorcery
witchcraft
wizardry

witch

fairy godmother

leprechaun

princess

giant

Fee fi fo fum

fairy

dragon

prince

king queen

goblin

pixie

unicorn

gnome   toadstool

horse and carriage

elf

Fairy-tale characters may...
cast spells
change shape
come to the rescue
fight battles
grant wishes
solve riddles
vanish into thin air

The good characters are...
beautiful
brave
generous
gentle
handsome
kind
pretty

The bad characters are...
creepy
cunning
evil
menacing
sinister
ugly
wicked

giant
hulk
ogre

wizard
magician
sorcerer

cast a spell
bewitch
enchant
transform

Wizards and witches use a...
cloak of invisibility
crystal ball
flying broomstick
magic potion
magic wand

Wizards say...
Abracadabra!
Hocus pocus!
Shazam!

Fairy-tale places
castle
cave
cavern
cottage
dungeon
forest
lake
maze
palace
tower
tunnel
wood

Hey presto!

spell
charm
curse

bat

book of spells

100 Top Spells

zap!

cauldron

wizard

Magic potions...
boil
bubble
simmer
fizz
froth

Potion ingredients
bat's wing
dragon's blood
snake's tongue
unicorn's horn

Pirates and treasure

Pirates can be...
bloodthirsty
bold
brutal
cruel
daring
fearless
fierce
greedy
menacing
reckless
swashbuckling

Pirates may...
board ships
bury treasure
explore desert
   islands
fire cannons
force prisoners to
   walk the plank
go ashore
keep a lookout
scrub the deck
sing sea shanties
take prisoners

steal
loot
plunder
raid
rob

Shiver me timbers!

lookout

telescope

Jolly Roger/skull and crossbones

sail

Yo ho ho!

plank

cabin boy

cannon

figurehe

anchor

message in a bottle

Pirate ships may...
brave the storm
cross the ocean
ride the waves
run aground

In a storm, a ship may ...
groan
shudder
sink/capsize

mast

crow's nest

captain

rigging

shark-infested waters

eye patch

hook

goblet
chalice
cup

peg leg
wooden leg

chest
trunk

cutlass

crown
coronet
tiara

gold coins

treasure
booty
bounty
loot
riches

jewels
gems
precious stones

coins
ducats
doubloons
pieces of eight

Types of jewelery
bangles
beads
bracelets
brooches
earrings
necklaces
rings

Precious stones
amber
amethyst
diamond
emerald
pearl
ruby
sapphire
turquoise

Treasure can be ...
dazzling
gleaming
glittering
inlaid with gems
sparkling

Or it can be ...
dusty
grimy
rusty
tarnished
worthless

In space

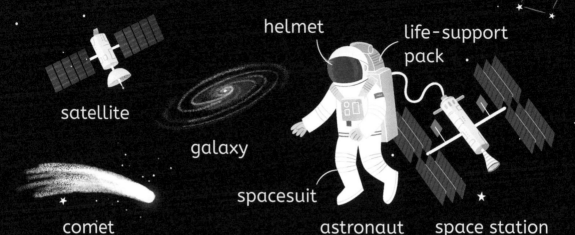

constellation

helmet

life-support pack

satellite

galaxy

spacesuit

comet

astronaut

space station

spaceship
rocket
spacecraft

Other spacecraft
moon buggy
spacelab
space shuttle

Other space words
Milky Way
universe

Spaceships may ...
blast off
crash land
cruise
lift off
orbit the Earth
reenter the
  Earth's
  atmosphere
zoom through
  space

Astronauts may ...
contact mission
  control
conduct
  experiments
experience
  zero gravity
float
hover
moonwalk
spacewalk

Sun

Moon

asteroid belt

Solar system

Uranus

Mercury

Earth

Venus

Mars

Jupiter

Saturn

Neptune

planets

On a space adventure

flying saucer

volcano

dust storm

gas cloud

zoom!

whoosh!

zap!

laser gun

rocket

alien

crater

You might travel by ...
starship
teleporter

You might meet ...
androids
extraterrestrial
beings
Martians
shape shifters
space pirates

You might be ...
caught in an
intergalactic war
lost in deep space
stranded on a
distant planet
stuck in a
parallel universe
sucked into a
black hole
trapped in a force
field

Planets may be ...
airless
baking
barren
dusty
frozen
glowing
icy
rocky
teeming with life
uninhabited
windy

Ghosts and haunted houses

Ghostly sounds
bang
bump
clank
clatter
clink
crash
creak
groan
hammer
knock
moan
mutter
rattle
screech
sigh
sob
thud

cackle!

cape

full moon

broomstick

witch

cobweb

bats

spider

zombie

skeleton

coffin   vampire   tombstone

Ghostly sounds can be...	Ghosts may...	You may...
bloodcurdling	appear	be rooted to the spot
chilling	beckon	be scared out of your wits
creepy	drift	
eerie	float	cover your eyes
hair-raising	glide	hide
heart-stopping	haunt	run for your life
spine-chilling	hover	scream
weird	vanish	shudder
	waft	

ghost
ghoul
gremlin
poltergeist
spirit

wail!

creak!

Haunted houses
   can be ...
creepy
crumbling
dark
deserted
gloomy
menacing
moonlit
mysterious
neglected
rambling
shadowy
spooky

howl!

mist

yowl!

black cat

werewolf

In a haunted house
attic
cellar
dungeon
family portraits
four-poster bed
grandfather clock
library
locked door
looking glass

oak chest
paneled room
secret passageway
spiral staircase
stone steps
suit of armor
tower
trap door
turret

You may see
   or hear ...
banging windows
clanking chains
creaking
 floorboards
fluttering curtains
guttering candles
hidden laughter
muffled screams

Monsters

Monsters may be ...
curious
fire-breathing
friendly
greedy
one-eyed
slimy
smelly
spiteful

fierce
bloodthirsty
ferocious
rough
savage
violent

ugly
hideous
monstrous

Monster homes
bog
castle
cave
dungeon
forest
lake
swamp
well

Monsters may have ...

wrinkles

tangled hair

warts

spikes

scales

hairy toes

shaggy fur

fiery breath

webbed feet

Monsters may ...
belch   bellow
grumble   roar

slime

tentacles

Dinosaurs

Types of dinosaurs
brachiosaurus
diplodocus
iguanodon
stegosaurus
velociraptor

Dinosaurs may have ...
bony plates
leathery wings
pointed fangs
scaly skin

Dinosaurs may ...
attack
charge
chase
chomp
fight
hunt
kick
munch
pounce
rear up
snarl
snatch

Large dinosaurs may ...
lumber
plod
thunder

Small dinosaurs may ...
gallop
scamper
scuttle
trot

beak

pterosaur

lava

Volcanoes ...
erupt
rumble
send out
  clouds of ash
smoke
smolder

club tail

roar!

ankylosaurus

claws

horn

ferns

tyrannosaurus

triceratops

Adventure words

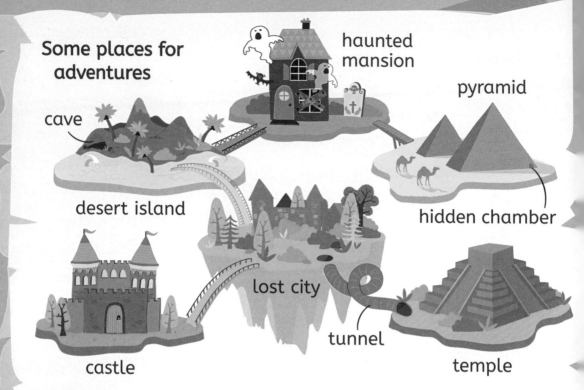

Some places for adventures

cave

desert island

haunted mansion

pyramid

hidden chamber

lost city

tunnel

castle

temple

Castles may be ...
awe-inspiring
crumbling
gloomy
magnificent
ruined

Lost cities may be ...
abandoned
deserted
empty
forgotten

Caves may be ...
damp
echoing
freezing
icy cold
pitch-black

Cave walls may be ...
dripping
gleaming
glistening
slimy
slippery

Hidden chambers may be ...
airless
cramped
dark
musty
shadowy
stuffy

Tunnels may be ...
narrow
twisting
winding

sliding panel

pillar

secret passage

urn

tomb
coffin
grave

mummy

statue

scarab
beetle

hieroglyphics
picture writing

**Adventures
may be ...**

action-packed
amazing
dangerous
exciting
frightening
incredible
spine-chilling
terrifying
thrilling

**Some adventure
clues**

chart
coded message
diary
inscription
manuscript
map
photograph
sealed letter
secret code

**You will need
to be ...**

adventurous
brave
curious
daring
determined
inquisitive

treasure
chest

You may need ...

camera

codebook

binoculars

survival kit

notebook

compass

rope ladder

flashlight

pocketknife

Knights and castles

Knights lived...
in medieval times
in the Middle Ages

joust
tournament

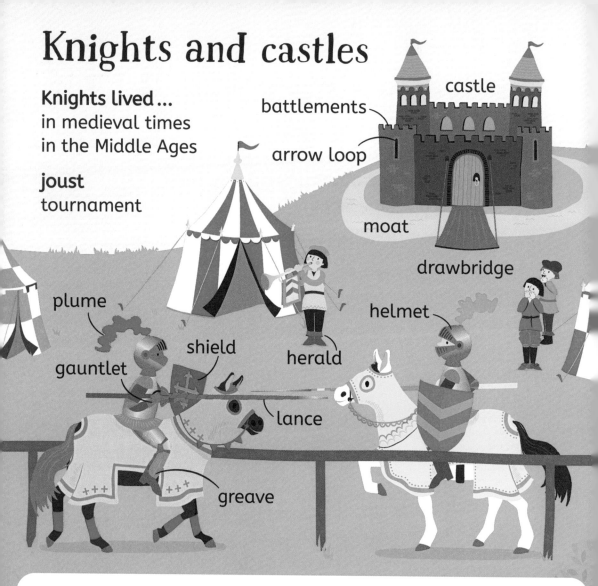

castle

battlements

arrow loop

moat

drawbridge

helmet

plume

shield

herald

gauntlet

lance

greave

Places in a castle
bedchamber
chapel
courtyard
dungeon
gatehouse
great hall
keep (central
   fortress)
kitchen
watchtower

Knights wore ...
chainmail
a suit of armor

Knights' weapons
battle-ax
broadsword
dagger
morning star
   (spiked ball
   on a chain)

**Battle weapons
   and equipment**
arrows
battering ram
boiling oil
catapult
crossbow
longbow
pikestaff
siege tower
slingshot

At a feast

feast
banquet

coats of arms

tapestry

piper

fiddler

minstrels' gallery

page

lord

lady

high table

platter

goblet

jester
fool

acrobat

juggler

dancer

Food at a feast	Guests at a feast	Lords and ladies wore ...
boar's head	bishop	cloak/mantle
boiled custard	king	coronet
jellied eels	knight	fur-lined gown
marzipan swan	noble	headdress
pastry castle	priest	hood
pigeon pie	prince	robe/dress
roast heron	princess	tights/hose
roast peacock	queen	tunic
salted fish	sheriff	veil
venison	squire	

Word finder

Do you want to find an alternative for a particular word? This word finder will show you where to find other interesting words to use in its place.

a

afraid
see **scared**, 17

amazed
see **surprised**, 16

amazing
see **nice**, 6

angry, 16

announce, 14

annoyed
see **grumpy**, 17

answer, 14

anxious
see **worried**, 16

applaud, 49

arrive, 42

ask, 14

astonished
see **surprised**, 16

attractive
see **good-looking**, 10

b

bad, 6

bad-tempered
see **grumpy**, 17

bang (door), 81

beach, 75

beautiful
see **good-looking**, 10
see **nice**, 6

beg see **ask**, 14

big, 7

bite, 55

blue, 8

boastful
see **proud**, 19

boiling
see **hot**, 76

bored, 16

boring, 47

bottom (mountain), 68

bouncy
see **lively**, 19

brainy
see **clever**, 19

brave, 19

bright (color), 8

brilliant
see **bright**, 8

build, 30

busy (city), 32

c

calm
(person) 18
(music) 50

car
(types), 36, 37

caring
see **nice**, 6

carry, 15

catch, 53

chat
see **talk**, 14

cheap, 34

cheer
see applaud, 49

cheerful, 18

chest
(treasure), 85

chew
see bite, 55
see eat, 26

chop
(food), 27

clap
see applaud, 49

clean (house), 29

clear
(see-through),
31

clever, 19

climb, 15

cloudy, 76

clumsy, 19

cold
(food and
drink), 25
(weather), 76

comment
see mention, 14

conceited
see proud, 19

concentrate on
see think about,
14

confident, 19

confused, 16

cook, 27

cool
see cold, 76

crash
see bang, 81

crazy, 18

creepy
see frightening,
47

cross
see angry, 16
see grumpy, 17

crowded
see busy, 32

crown, 85

cruel
see unkind, 18

cry, 17

curious
see nosy, 19

d

daring
see brave, 19

dark
(color), 8

deceitful
see dishonest, 18

decide
see think
about, 14

deep
(sound), 81

delicious, 26

deliver
see give, 15

depressed
see sad, 16

depressing
see sad, 47

deserted
see empty, 32

difficult
see hard, 45

dirty
(city), 32
(clothes), 13

disgusting, 26

good, 6

good-looking, 10

grab
  see **catch**, 53
  see **hold**, 15
  see **take**, 15

grave
  see **tomb**, 93

gray, 8

great
  see **nice**, 6

green, 8

grin
  see **smile**, 17

grumpy, 17

guess
  see **think**, 14

gurgle
  see **splash**, 81

h

hand over
  see **give**, 15

handsome
  see **good-looking**, 10

happy, 16

hard
  (material), 31
  (game), 45

hate, 17

healthy, 18

hear, 21

heavy
  see **big**, 7

help yourself
  see **take**, 15

helpful
  see **nice**, 6

high
  (sound), 81

hilarious
  see **funny**,
   19, 47

hill, 64

hit, 53

hold, 15

honest, 18

horrible
  see **bad**, 6

hot
  (food and drink), 25
  (weather), 76

huge
  see **big**, 7

hurt
  see **upset**, 17

i

imagine
  see **think**, 14

important
  (decision)
  see **big**, 7

inquisitive
  see **nosy**, 19

intelligent
  see **clever**, 19

invent
  see **think up**, 14

irritable
  see **grumpy**, 17

j

jewels, 85

jingle
  see **ring**, 81

jolly
  see **cheerful**, 18

jump, 15

a
b
c
d
e
f
g
h
i
j
k
l
m
n
o
p
q
r
s
t
u
v
w
x
y
z

noisy
   see **loud**, 81

nosy, 19

notice
   see **feel**, 21
   see **hear**, 21
   see **see**, 21
   see **taste**, 21

o

obedient (dog), 54

old, 18

orange, 8

p

pale
   see **light**, 8

path, 64

pattern (types), 9

peaceful
   see **calm**, 18, 50

peak
   see **top**, 68

pick
   see **take**, 15

picky, 19

place
   see **put**, 15

pink, 8

point out
   see **mention**, 14

pointed, 9

polite, 18

press
   see **push**, 15

pretty
   see **good-looking**, 10

proud, 19

pull, 15

purple, 8

push, 15

put, 15

puzzled
   see **confused**, 16

q

quickly, 26

quiet, 81

r

rainy, 76

recover
   see **get better**, 23

red, 8

refreshing, 25

relaxed
   see **calm**, 18

reply
   see **answer**, 14

revolting
   see **bad**, 6

ridiculous
   see **funny**, 19, 47

ring (bell), 81

roar
   see **shout**, 81

rob see **steal**, 84

rough
   see **fierce**, 90

round (shape), 9

rude, 18

run, 15

a
b
c
d
e
f
g
h
i
j
k
l
m
n
o
p
q
r
s
t
u
v
w
x
y
z

stand
see **put**, 15

steal, 84

steamy, 76

storm, 78

story (types), 45

strong
(person), 18
(material), 31

stuck-up
see **proud**, 19

stunning
see **nice**, 6

sunny
see **fine**, 76

suppose
see **think**, 14

surprised, 16

swerve
see **dodge**, 53

t

talk, 14

talk loudly, 14

talk quietly, 14

take, 15

take care of
see **look after**, 23

tall, 7

taste, 21

tense
see **nervous**, 18
see **worried**, 16

terrified
see **scared**, 17

terrifying
see **frightening**, 47

thick
(hair), 11

thin
(hair), 11
(person), 7

think, 14

think about, 14

think up, 14

thrilled
see **excited**, 16

throw, 53

tidy, 29

tight (clothes), 13

tiny, 7

tired, 17

tomb, 93

top
(mountain), 68

touch
see **feel**, 21

tough
see **strong**, 31

treasure, 85

truthful
see **honest**, 18

try
see **taste**, 21

tug
see **pull**, 15

u

ugly, 90

unhappy
see **sad**, 16

unimportant
(mistake)
see **small**, 7

unkind, 18

a b c d e f g h i j k l m n o p q r s t u v w x y z

A B C D E F G H I J K L M N O P Q R S T U V W X Y Z

untidy
see **messy**, 29

upset, 17

V

vacation, 42

vain
see **proud**, 19

vast
see **big**, 7

vegetable
(types), 25

violent
see **fierce**, 90

violet, 8

W

walk, 15

wander
see **walk**, 15

warm
(food and
drink), 25

watch
see **look**, 21

weak
(person), 18
(material), 31
(weather), see
fine, 76

well
see **healthy**, 18

weep
see **cry**, 17

whisper
see **talk quietly**,
14

wicked
see **bad**, 6

wide
see **big**, 7

wild
see **naughty**, 19

windy, 76

wizard, 83

wonder
see **think**, 14

wonderful
see **nice**, 6

woods
(forest), 64

work
see **job**, 44

work out
see **think about**,
14

worn out
see **tired**, 17

worried, 16

Y

yell
see **shout**, 81

yellow, 8

young, 18

Americanization editor: Carrie Armstrong